Faith is to believe what you do not see; the reward of this is to see what you believe.

- Saint Augustine

_____

_____

_____

_____

_____

_____

_____

_____

_____

_____

_____

_____

_____

_____

_____

_____

_____

_____

_____

_____

And we know that in all things God works for the good of those who love him, who have been called according to his purpose.

- Romans 8:28

_____

_____

_____

_____

_____

_____

_____

_____

_____

_____

_____

_____

_____

_____

_____

_____

_____

_____

_____

_____

_____

God loves each of us as if there were only one
of us.

- Saint Augustine

God gave us the gift of life; it is up to us
to give ourselves the gift of living well.

- Voltaire

_____

_____

_____

_____

_____

_____

_____

_____

_____

_____

_____

_____

_____

_____

_____

_____

_____

_____

_____

_____

_____

So do not fear, for I am with you; do not be dismayed,
for I am your God. I will strengthen you and help you;
I will uphold you with my righteous right hand.

- Isaiah 41:10

Taste and see that the Lord is good; blessed is the one who takes refuge in him.

- Psalms 34:8

We have different gifts, according to the grace given to each of us. If your gift is prophesying, then prophesy in accordance with your faith; if it is serving, then serve; if it is teaching, then teach.

- Romans 12:6-7

_____

_____

_____

_____

_____

_____

_____

_____

_____

_____

_____

_____

_____

_____

_____

_____

_____

_____

_____

**You have made us for yourself, O Lord, and our
hearts are restless until they rest in you.**

- Saint Augustine

_____
_____
_____
_____
_____
_____
_____
_____
_____
_____
_____
_____
_____
_____
_____
_____
_____
_____
_____
_____

For God is not unjust so as to overlook your work
and the love that you have shown for his name in
serving the saints, as you still do.

- Hebrews 6:10

_____

_____

_____

_____

_____

_____

_____

_____

_____

_____

_____

_____

_____

_____

_____

_____

_____

_____

_____

Remember your leaders who first taught you the word of God. Think of all the good that has come from their lives, and trust the Lord as they do.

- Hebrews 13:7

_____

_____

_____

_____

_____

_____

_____

_____

_____

_____

_____

_____

_____

_____

_____

_____

_____

_____

_____

_____

_____

_____

Be on your guard; stand firm in the
faith; be courageous; be strong.

- 1 Corinthians 16:13

May the God of hope fill you with all joy and peace as you trust in him, so that you may over-flow with hope by the power of the Holy Spirit.

- Romans 15:13

Made in the USA
Monee, IL
27 November 2022

18759447R00056